# Chatting with 100

BLAISE FORET

Copyright © 2016 Blaise Foret Publications

All rights reserved.

ISBN: **1535284021**

To my wife, Christina. You are my delight.

# CONTENTS

|   | Introduction | 1 |
|---|---|---|
| 1 | Know Your Audience | 6 |
| 2 | Make Your Point | 15 |
| 3 | Find Your Message | 19 |
| 4 | Know Yourself | 24 |
| 5 | Share Your Story | 30 |
| 6 | Speaking with Authenticity and Confidence | 35 |
| 7 | Preparation is Everything | 42 |
| 8 | Conclusion: Tips and Tricks | 71 |

# ACKNOWLEDGMENTS

I'd like to thank Christina for constantly encouraging me and inspiring me to do big things. Thanks to my Dad, Randy Foret, for doing the first read through and convincing me that this book was solid content that would help many people. And thank you to all who pick up this book and then use the ideas within to help you express your ideas that will change the world!

# Introduction

Public speaking sounds so intimidating to most people. Many people when asked if they want to be a public speaker would say, "Absolutely not." But when asked if they want to influence or impact multiple people in their lifetime they would say, "Of course!"

Public speaking is a profession for some- but most of you are not reading this because you want to make it your profession. Most of you are here because you have a message, you have a story, and you want to impact the world with it.

You are here because you want to change the world. You're here because you are a passionate person with a powerful message that needs to be communicated effectively to many people. Most people in their lifetime will be called upon to give some sort of public presentation. Whether it's at a family gathering when asked to say something around the table, at a small group meeting of 10-20 people who want to hear your story, or at a large event speaking to 100 or more, I want you to feel the exact same way about your ability to communicate. I want you to feel comfortable, calm, and confident in the fact that what you are going to say will 1) make sense to your listeners and 2) impact their lives in a meaningful way.

That's what **Chatting with 100** is all about.

Imagine taking the enjoyable atmosphere of meeting a friend for coffee or hanging with a group of your favorite people for dinner and translating that to a public speaking venue of 100 or more. What does it feel like to grab coffee with friends? Are you uncomfortable? Are you nervous to share your thoughts with them? Are you scared of being part of the conversation?

For most of you, the answer is *of course not!* And if some of you would say *yes* to that question, then don't worry- this book will help you too!

No matter what stage you are currently at in your public communication skills, this book will help take you to the next level.

I can remember my first public speech at 15 years old. It was a "How to" speech all about skateboarding. I fumbled through it, constantly revealing my insecurity by shuffling around and trying to rush through it. But I do remember one thing in particular- I knew what I was talking about so I had a small sense of confidence because of that.

Fast-forward a year later- I had a deep and very impacting spiritual experience that influenced my life in a profound way. It was after having this experience that I realized I wanted to share it with as many people as possible. I hadn't spent much time in front of people but I knew that eventually, I wanted to share my life and message with as many people as possible. A few months later I was asked by a friend to share my story at a youth conference.

I didn't have any formal training or coaching, just a message that I wanted to share and a love for people. I said "um" and "but" around 93 times in 25 minutes- but that didn't matter. I was hooked. I had to impact and influence people using my voice- and I had to speak to as many people as I could.

I found a niche for myself at churches and ministries over the next 15 years and learned the **art of audible influence** through the school of personal experience and hard knocks. During those years, my thoughts and views morphed and changed and grew and expanded, but one thing has remained the same: my passion to express those thoughts to those around me in a way that will positively inspire them. I've been flown to conferences to speak to groups of 1,000 or more, and driven across the country to share my story with a living room full of 10 people. It's all the same to me at this point- I really do find myself feeling exactly the same about both groups.

Why? Because I've learned to chat with 100 in the same way I chat with 10- and with 10 using the same values and principles I use in chatting with one.

I feel comfortable, calm, and confident. I enjoy my time with 1, 10, 100, or 1,000 or more- and I see similar results in the lives of the listeners regardless of the size of the audience.

How does this happen? Well, that's what I hope to show you in this book. Sit back, relax, and let's dive in.

# CHATTING WITH 100

## 1 KNOW YOUR AUDIENCE

Recently, my wife and I stopped to pick up groceries and had the most interesting experience with the clerk. I'd met this guy a number of times. He is probably the most charismatic personality I've ever seen behind a cash register. Tall, bearded, green eyes, big smile, and an even bigger personality. He started chatting with us as we were checking out and told us all about his hip-hop group and how they were the number one group in the region. It was actually very engaging and entertaining to chat with him. But as soon as we walked out of the store we found ourselves just giggling and saying, "Yeah, we probably won't go to that show."

As I evaluated the conversation I realized that not once did the young man ask us if we *liked* hip-hop nor did he find out any of our interests at all. He also didn't say anything convincing to us about why we should go to the show. Really, he just talked about himself and his group the entire time.

<u>He didn't know his audience</u> and therefore, was unable to convince his audience.

I'm not going to overcomplicate this point. I'm going to do my best to keep it super simple- because it is!

Here's the key question: WHO ARE YOU TALKING TO?

When you are chatting with one person, you naturally find a way to relate with them. You look for a common denominator as you listen and engage the person in front of you. We speak differently to different people in our lives. You talk to your parents in a different way than you talk with your kids. You talk with your spouse in a different manner than you chat with your friends- at least I hope you do.

Why? Because the relationship is on a different level and the information that you know about that person dictates how you approach them and the information you share with them.

Here are a few things to pay attention to when thinking about your audience:

Are your listeners apart of a group or are they random attendees?

What's the average age?

What's the culture?

What are their interests?

Are they on social media? What platforms specifically?

What media do they intake?

Do they have kids? Do they have grandkids?

Are they rich? Poor? Middle class?

Are they mostly conservative? Religious? Socially liberal?

All of this **MATTERS**.

Years ago I was speaking to a college in Minnesota and I used the phrase "MTV Generation" when talking about them. I got the funniest look from those in the room and I wasn't sure why. I realized later on that I was relating to these college students, who were almost 10 years younger than me, as though I was still in college. MTV was popular when I was 20, but was not popular at all among these students. Looking back on that moment, I realize that I made myself look a little old and out of touch. Which of course, is never a good approach.

I quickly learned that I needed to know my audience in order to use phrases that they used. Knowing this information has a huge impact on whether or not your audience will take you seriously.

Knowing your audience helps you understand what they need. Know them and study their need and know exactly how you are going to meet that need in your presentation.

What do they need?

And how are you going to meet that need with the information you are presenting to them? Do they even know that they need it?

Sometimes they don't know that they need what you have. But if you can get to know them well enough, you can appeal to a need that they do not know they have. Let me explain...

Remember the grocery store rapper?

If this guy had taken a moment to get to know Christina and I then he would have found out that we have one of the largest online community's in our city. What could he have done with that information? Well, I guess he'll never know.

Not only could he have used that information to his own advantage (i.e. creating connections) but he could have found out what we were involved in and what already interested us and- here's the key- used that information to convince us that we need to be interested in hip-hop and ultimately get us to come to his show.

All of this translates to chatting with 100. When you know your audience, you know their needs and then you can better craft your presentation to convince them that you have what they need.

**Charisma is not enough.** This guy was so excited and charismatic that it made us think that we might actually go to his show. But when we left, we forgot about it because he didn't say anything that convinced us to be there. Charisma can catch someone up in a moment while they are listening to a speech, but detailed and curated information presented in a skilled, crafted, and relatable way is what will make people want to be a part of something even after the hype of the meeting is over.

**Here are a few ways to get to know your audience:**

-Research the place where you will be speaking. Know some of the history of the city, state, organization, small group, etc.

-Show up early and shake hands with people. You don't have to hide away in the *Green Room* while you're waiting for the meeting to begin. Build trust by meeting people, asking for names, finding out a few pieces of key information from your attendees that you can use during your speech to relate with the audience.

-When meeting people beforehand, have a conversation with one or two of the attendees about the topic you'll be presenting. Find out their knowledge of the topic and where they might be lacking in understanding. That way you can curate certain parts of your speech to their need by highlighting those parts during the speech.

*For example: "I was chatting with John from Knoxville before the event today and he shared with me about his journey as a small business owner. He said his greatest need is online marketing- how many of you have had this same struggle?"*

You just showed the audience that you are personable by remembering someone's name from the audience and the details of the conversation. This does two things: 1) Builds trust with the crowd because it makes others feel like you would remember their name as well 2) Shows that you care about the people enough to show up early and talk with some of the attendees.

Obviously, you don't always gain information that you can use during your talk. But the more short conversations you can have with attendees the more opportunity you will find to genuinely meet people you enjoy. That will create a more natural means of sharing that conversation from the front when you are speaking. The more genuine you are about meeting people and caring about them the easier it will be to use their names from the front without it feeling forced or disingenuous.

So get out there. Meet people. Learn your audience and get to know them! They are in fact the reason you are doing what you are doing as a public speaker. You care about people and you want them to be impacted by what you have to say. So go meet your people!

## 2 MAKE YOUR POINT

Last month I was in Greenville, SC and had some work to get done during the day. I stopped by a small cigar lounge / coffee shop in town hoping to focus and knock out a few tasks. A few minutes later a woman walked in and started talking to pretty much anyone who would listen to her. She rattled on about this and that for the next hour. She spoke to one man for around 30 minutes. The man stood up picked up his bags and began walking away slowly- all while the woman continued on as though he was still sitting there listening. When he disappeared, she didn't skip a beat. She turned to someone else and continued talking. Needless to say, I put in my headphones so that I wouldn't be the next victim.

What's my point? Exactly- **what is my point!?**

Some folks have no problem standing in front of people and talking. But their ability to go on long drawn out rabbit trails is just as strong as their confidence to speak in front of people. By the way, that is not a compliment.

Public speaking is not about public speaking- **it's about public influence.** Are you taking people somewhere? Are you bringing them to a crescendo? Do they know it? Can they sense it?

I'm not saying that you can't tell stories along the way- that's actually a powerful part of public speaking (story telling, I mean). But every story, every rabbit trail, and every content filled conglomeration of seconds and minutes must all build up to the main point. Ask yourself, "What is my point? What am I actually trying to say and if the story I'm about to rabbit trail into doesn't fit the main point, then should I really tell it?"

As a young speaker I had this problem. I mean... I really had this problem.

I would be on my way to making a powerful and impacting point- a crescendo of sorts- when suddenly, I would say a certain word or specific phrase that would launch my mind into a daydream or a memory of a story that I just knew would be hilarious to tell. So there I went, off into oblivion, and often with no hope of return. As I got further into the story I would lose my main point and end it with, "I'm not sure why I told that story..."

Not the best way to make a point. And I'm not saying you can't recover from that moment- and a good speaker will definitely find a way back on track- but you can avoid a ton of headaches (and people getting up and walking out of your talk) by sticking with your main point and avoiding constant rabbit trails.

SO what's my point? My point is that you need to know your point and stick with it. I'll talk more about this when we get to our "Preparation" section.

## 3 FIND YOUR MESSAGE

You might be sitting there thinking, "No one is asking me to speak at their venue or event."

That's the wrong thought. Your job is not to worry about who is asking you to speak somewhere, but your job is to find your message. When you have a message worth sharing then you can start thinking about where to share it. The truth is, we all have a message, but not everyone takes the time to pinpoint their message. Here are a few questions to ask yourself when you are finding your message:

What makes you tick?

What makes you excited?

What topic do you find yourself discussing with your close friends?

What topic do you think about most when you are alone?

What topic do you know the most about?

There could be a number of different answers to each of those questions. Let's narrow it down a bit.

What topic or story are you passionate about making sure others know about? If you had only one chance to speak only one message for the masses- what would it be about?

Answering those questions doesn't always mean you will only talk about one issue or share one message your entire life. The point of answering those questions is to help you narrow down your focus away from topics that don't matter much to you and onto topics that you really care about. Because if you don't care about what you are sharing from the front of the stage, then your audience won't care either.

I remember when my wife and I first moved to North Carolina. All she talked about was making friends and connecting with a positive and artistic community. So she took to social media to make it happen- and make it happen she did. To the tune of 14K followers on Instagram in 10 months, backyard dinners all around town, and creative talks in local breweries with over 100 attendees.

When I saw this happen, it was clear to me what her message was. Now, she spends time blogging and speaking to large audiences about creating genuine connection and community via social media.

This is what gets her out of bed in the morning. This is what makes her tick. This is what drives her. This is her message.

When I was 15 years old, I had a profound spiritual experience that impacted my life. That's all I could think about and all that I wanted to talk about. I knew pretty quickly that this was my message was to the world.

Why? Because this is what I think about when I don't have to. This is why I wake up in the morning. This is what I was made to communicate- this is my message.

Can you have more than *one* message? Of

course! Just make sure that what you are sharing actually matters to you when you are up there speaking to others about it!

## 4 KNOW YOURSELF

Standing in front of people can be intimidating.

Public speakers are just like the rest of the world. They struggle with the same issues and insecurities. They just have to overcome them in order to stand in front of people and remain confident and secure.

Frustrations, insecurities, worries, and fears affect the best of us and cause us to question ourselves. It doesn't matter what faith tradition you are currently a part of or whether you practice yoga or crossfit. Those things don't always produce confidence and security.

I know Christians who live in continual frustration that they aren't good enough, new age spiritualists who live with deep anger problems, and agnostics who are confused about life. When it comes to knowing yourself, especially in context to public speaking, it's less about a religious framework, and more about what you believe about yourself.

I'm not here to tell you what to believe about the divine or spirituality, but I am here to tell you what you must believe about yourself if you are going to be a confident, comfortable, and effective public speaker.

When you look in the mirror, what do you see? When you look into your own eyes, what do you see?

For me, I have found it to be invaluable to see myself as a product of perfect and powerful creativity. I see myself as a unique and divine expression of something greater than myself. Self confidence cannot be found only in self- but must go deeper. We are all deep wells of mystery and untapped understanding. To embrace the mystical side of ourselves doesn't have to mean we become guru's who live on the backside of a desert, or religious nuts who believe the end is near. It just means that we simply embrace mystery and stand in awe of a greater reality.

You might not agree with me on spiritual matters, but most can at least agree with me that humanity, and you in particular, are absolutely amazing.

Positivity is the key to seeing this truth.

Anyone can find fault in themselves, but it takes a courageous person to see the beauty in themselves and to embrace it.

When it comes to weakness and imperfection- it truly takes a person of confidence to embrace their weaknesses, own up to them, and not be afraid to laugh at them with confidence.

Listen, I am 5'6" (on a good day). That is below average for men my age. I used to have a very hard time with that in the early years of speaking and so I would overcompensate by being louder or more "in your face" when I spoke. But this wasn't my true persona- it was just a cover up for what I perceived to be a weakness.

Over the years, I became more accepting of myself and learned to just enjoy the fact that I'm short and really own it. I'm 33 years old and I really don't care what people think about my height or size. I just get a kick out of the fact that people I meet on the street think I'm a 20 year old college student!

Here's the thing- if you can embrace your so-called "weakness" then you can use it for your advantage. For example, when I look out into the audience and see people in their 50's and 60's I immediately know what they are thinking- "Who is this kid on the stage and why am I here listening to a 20 year old?"

I often start off my talk with a short jab at myself and just laugh it off with them. *"It's great to be here and see all of your smiling faces. I've been speaking and sharing my story since I was 16 years old. I know that some of you think that must have been last year, but I promise, I'm much older than I look."*

This always eases the crowd, makes them smile and giggle a bit, and gives me the feeling like they are no longer wondering about my age.

This is something I do because I realize that it's a question I get all of the time from my audience. But don't make this into a formula- because that phrase might not work for you *if you really are only a teenager*.

The point is, find your place of insecurity, accept yourself as you are, and use it for your advantage! Often times, the very thing we are most insecure about can become the greatest gift to you and be the bridge for an opportunity to connect with your audience on levels you may not have been able to do so otherwise.

Be thankful for who you are. Be confident that you are a unique gift to this world. Your voice matters because your life matters. This is one of the first steps to knowing yourself and having the ability to confidently stand in front of anyone and share your story.

For more on this, check out my blog, or my book "It is Finished, Why You Can Quit Religion and Trust in Jesus". In it, I talk a lot about our value as human beings and finding our identity in something greater than our insecurities.

## 5 SHARE YOUR STORY

The most impacting public presentations happen when someone goes from giving flat facts and interesting information to sharing personal stories of failure and victory.

Anyone can spout off information about a topic with enough study, preparation, and note reading. But no one can tell your story the way that you can.

This is huge. I want you to actually say this with me:

**"NO ONE CAN TELL MY STORY THE WAY I CAN."**

Some of you might be thinking, "Well, I don't have a story."

Yes you do. That's why you are reading this book. It's because somewhere on the inside you feel the deep desire to communicate something of impact to an audience. Somewhere deep down you know that there are people out there who need what you have to offer. I want to propose that the very inclination to become a more excellent and relevant communicator is just **your unique story wanting to be told.**

No one else has ever lived a day in your shoes.

So no one else can tell your story the way that you can.

Who you are today is a product of your story.

Your story is simply the life of you.

What have you gone through?

Where did you grow up?

What was your family like? (many of us could write a novel based on that alone)

What were some of the challenges you faced growing up?

How did you overcome those challenges?

What challenges are you currently facing?

How are you overcoming them today?

What are some of your greatest memories?

What are some of your greatest victories?

Who were your friends?

Who are your friends today?

Who has impacted you the most? Why? What did they say or do?

What are a few life lessons you've learned after living in your shoes?

If you could go back and speak to yourself as a teenager, young adult, or middle-aged person, what would you say? What advice would you give yourself?

Answering these questions will be like taking a tour back into your life story. Many of you who think that you don't have a powerful story will find that in fact, you have a story that is worth sharing and could be helpful for many people.

One of the biggest problems I find is that people tend to compare their stories to the stories of others who seem to have more dramatic life events. Just because you weren't a drug dealer at 5 years old who had a dramatic life change at

20 and are now a family man and philanthropist who helps orphans in Uganda does not mean that your story is not powerful! I love a good sappy story. I love a good dramatic story. But the truth is, those stories aren't the norm. And though they can be impacting and inspiring, most people can't fully relate to them.

Most people are normal folks who have been through a lot of normal life events. But those normal events can be inspiring when we tell the details of our story and what we have learned along the way.

Take the next 2-3 hours to answer those questions above. Some of you might find yourself writing a novel- and that's totally okay. When you actually give yourself the time to reflect on these life events and life lessons you will realize that you have a lot to say. And as you reflect on your life, you might just find that you have a life message that you need to share with the world!

BLAISE FORET

## 6 AUTHENTICITY AND CONFIDENCE

My desire is that each person reading this material would have the same confidence standing in front of 100's of people that they have when they are sitting down having coffee with a close friend.

How does it feel to sit with a close friend?

You feel authentic, comfortable, confident secure, happy, free, informed, relaxed, and excited to chat with them about whatever is on your mind.

THIS IS EXACTLY HOW YOU SHOULD FEEL WHEN STANDING UP TO SPEAK TO 100 OR MORE PEOPLE.

The people who are listening to your talk should not dictate your security or confidence.

This is the most important point of this entire book.

Almost anyone can stand up in front of 100 people and read a page or two of notes. Information is available for free on Wikipedia so anyone can be an expert on anything after an hour on the Internet! But people don't come to an event to hear someone who can spout some information in an impersonal way. They come to an event because they want the presence of a live person with a real story giving them real information that has been experienced first hand.

There's a substance that can almost be felt when you are listening to someone who is speaking from experience. It's almost tangible.

Even if you are not a popular or famous speaker, people will listen when they feel that tangible substance on your content and when they see the confidence with which it's delivered. They may not know why they are listening to you at first, but after they hear you speak, it will be perfectly clear to them that you are the reason they came to this event. Your story and your style is what they needed to hear. The information given from your unique perspective and shared with your unique personality is what people will be excited about. It's not your ability to never say *"um"* or *"and uh"* during your talk that is going to inspire and motivate people.

If you know your stuff and are actually excited about it- and that comes across in your talk, then it doesn't matter how many speaking *no no's* you commit, you will impact your listeners and they will want to hear you again! People want to hear someone who is real. Someone who knows what they are talking about. Someone who isn't insecure, but cares that their listeners are deeply impacted by what's being spoken.

You have to change your thinking when it comes to being a speaker. You are not only a speaker, but you are an influencer. As soon as people enter your sphere of influence, they are your audience. You own the stage. You own the room. They are there because it was ordained that they would be there to hear what you have to say. If 25 people showed up to your event, then congratulations, you just made 25 new friends. You are about to chat with these 25 people and connect with them over a topic that you know they need more information about. And they need YOUR PERSPECTIVE. And they need YOUR VOICE to tell them about it.

This might sound prideful or arrogant, but it's not. It's actually true humility.

This is an identity thing.

You might still be thinking, "That's easy for you to say, Blaise. 100's of people show up to your meetings."

That's actually not true.

Last month I spoke on Saturday night to 13 people.

The very next morning I spoke to a room full of 250 people.

But guess what? My confidence didn't waiver. I spoke to the 13 in the same way I'd speak to 250. With the same passion and love and intensity and desire to change their lives. Of course I catered my message to those in attendance, but my driving passion and desire didn't change. I knew that I was supposed to be there to speak the words in my heart and they were supposed to be there to hear those words and be impacted, challenged, encouraged, and changed by them.

Some of you are just beginning your speaking career. Others might be many years into speaking to 1000's of people. And others might be looking to prepare one speech and that's why you or picked up this book.

It doesn't matter where you are at in your journey. You have the power and the ability to change people's lives!

One speech can change the world. One moment of sharing your passion and can affect someone's life in an earth shattering way.

It can change the trajectory of someone's life.

It can change the direction of an entire business.

It can convince someone to invest millions into your idea.

It can change the world!

Whether you are a traveling speaker with a message of your own, or you have been assigned by your boss or teacher to give a talk on a certain subject- you have the ability to own your subject, own your talk, and impact the crowd in a positive way! Change your thinking. You are there to connect with and impact the people in front of you- not just to spout off random information.

Never waste a moment with a microphone in your hand. That microphone is a weapon to induce pain on passive thinking and power into the hearts and minds of people in your audience. It's a tool to bring change and healing to the people who are there to listen. You have the power to connect with and change the lives of those in the audience. Make the most of every opportunity!

## 7 PREPARATION IS EVERYTHING

This section is where we get very practical. Some of you may have skipped immediately to this chapter because you are giving a speech tomorrow and just want the nuts and bolts of how to prepare. That's totally understandable! But don't underestimate the power of the philosophy behind your talk- which is what chapters 1-6 are all about. Once you have your thinking right, then the preparation comes much easier.

Okay. So let's dive in.

I'm going to share a few keys about how to

practically prepare for a public presentation. These principles can be used for any talk no matter what the length or audience. Here is a simple acronym that can help you quickly and effectively prepare a talk: T-E-A-M.

I love this acronym not only because it practically helps to prepare a speech, but also in that it reminds me I am working for the benefit of the audience. We are a team. I am there, on that stage, not to stroke my own ego, but to join the audience and give them valuable information that will in some way, impact and possibly change their lives forever.

If you can remember that key point of information, then it will change the way you experience your audience while on stage. If you can remember that you are on their **team** and they are on your **team**, then you can stand up in front of them with confidence and excitement instead of worry and fear.

Sure, some people will be judging you while you are on stage. But that doesn't mean they aren't on your team. They just don't know it yet! You are there, on that stage, to remind them that you are on their team and you have something valuable to give them. You are not up there to show people that you are more important than they are, but to be transparent, humble, and confident- and to empower people with the impacting information that you have to share with them. You are on their TEAM!

Okay. Now that you understand the value of a team mindset, let's talk about the practical planning stage of using the T-E-A-M acronym to prepare your speech.

T- Topic

E- Explanation

A- Assets

M- Master your Speech

**TEAM: Topic–**

This is your overall main point. What are you talking about and what do you want your audience to **know** or **do** after listening to you?

**TEAM: Explanation–**

These are a few points that breakdown and drive home your main topic. For example, in a one-page paper, these would be the opening sentences to your three paragraphs after your introduction and before your conclusion. I will explain more in the section below.

**TE<u>A</u>M: A**ssets–

These are the stories, quotes, statistics, and other resources that you would use to fill in and support your explanation.

**TEA<u>M</u>: M**aster your Speech –

This is the point where you spend time practicing over and over in order to become more familiar with the flow of your content and to master your speech.

Simple enough, right?

Now let me break those down a little further for you:

# Topic (Main Point)

This is either something that you have been asked to talk about or something that you want to talk about. You want this to be a short sentence that answers the questions: *What are you talking about, and what do you want your audience to do after listening to you?*

If you are preparing to talk to an investor about your business idea then it might look something like this:

*Topic — The Value of John's Coffee Shop and Why You Should Invest in It.*

If you were preparing a talk to a group of teenagers about finding and fulfilling their life calling then your topic would look something like this:

*Topic — Three Steps for Young People to Find and Fulfill Their Life Calling*

Figure out your topic, **who** you are talking to, and **what** you want them to **know** or **do** when they leave the talk.

<u>Don't over-think this part.</u> It should be simple. If you've been asked by someone to share something specific, then go with that topic. If you're holding your own event and want to share

something from your heart or a story from your life, then focus in on one topic and write it out in a simple sentence.

You need to be able to explain, in one sentence, what you want to say and what you want people to know. This might be hard to narrow down at first, but practice getting your topic laser focused and it will really help your preparation.

Think of your topic like the tip of the spear. Everything else in your talk will support the tip of that spear. Without the tip of the spear, you might hit your target, but you won't have a very powerful impact. If your topic is the point of the spear, then your <u>explanation</u> is the iron rod that you hold to throw the spear.

## Explanation (Sub-Points)

This section is very important. These are the points in the talk that you will use to <u>explain or support your main topic</u> and drive home your objective. If your topic is "How to Know that You are a Speaker" then your explanation will be something along these lines:

1. You love to share your opinions with others
2. You love to impact groups of people
3. People tell you that they like hearing your input
4. You would do it for free just because you enjoy it

Here are four points that support the main topic. Each of these points can be used to answer the question "How do I know that I'm a speaker?"

Obviously, there could be a number of answers to this question, but as the main speaker, it's your job to choose 2-4 points that you feel are the strongest points that will support your main objective.

Here is another example:

Topic: "Why You Should Move to Asheville, NC"

Explanation:

1. Asheville is the most non-judgmental and welcoming city in the South
2. Asheville is full of many outdoor activities for the whole family

3. Asheville is a city that is thriving and expanding

That is an example of a speech that is supported by three points. You can do this for any topic.

Choose your topic, then go write down 5-10 points that support your main topic. Then take the time to narrow down those 5-10 points into 3 or 4. Once you choose your 3-4 points that you feel are the most compelling and best explain your main point, that's when it's time to start building out the content of your speech.

## Assets

This is one of the most important parts of your preparation. It's easy for most people to come up with a **Topic**- and **Explanations**/sub points are not all that hard to find either. But the stories, quotes, and other resources that you use to build your points are where your talk becomes unique to you.

Your stories, quotes, statistics, etc. are your biggest assets to building out your content. If you are speaking on a topic that is near and dear to your heart (which I would highly recommend doing) then this stage of preparation will come more naturally. But if you are speaking on a topic that you are not very well versed in, which is necessary at times, then this part of your preparation will take a lot more time and research. Don't get discouraged! Put the time and effort into this stage of the game and you will be glad you did.

Let me give you an example of what an **asset** looks like and where it can be placed in a talk using the same topic and just one of the sub-points (explanations) we used above. I will use ***bold italics*** to insert teaching moments when I want to explain something to you (the reader) a little further.

"Why You Should Move to Asheville, NC"

1. Asheville is the most non-judgmental and welcoming city in the South

    <u>Asset 1</u> – Personal story: ("When I moved here I experienced _____.")

*This story will be anywhere from 3-5 minutes long and you can feel free to relax and ad-lib different parts of the story. You don't have to tell it exactly the same every time, just make sure that the story is really a part of you and that you are able to tell the story without any problems because it's something that impacted you in a deep and meaningful way. Your audience will pick up on your sincerity here and will enjoy listening to a story. Remember, everyone loves a good story.*

<u>Asset 2</u> – Quote from an influential Asheville local: "I love meeting new people when they move here. I'm so thankful for the many different types of people who are drawn to our city." *This quote doesn't stand alone. But you can use it while you are telling your story from asset 1 and insert it into the mix of the story. Or you can end your story with this quote. You want this quote to re-enforce the main explanation/sub-point in this section and it would be even better if it could also re-enforce and tie into your story somehow.*

**Remember, every asset is a building block to direct people back to and convince them of your overall main point. So yes, use stories, but don't let yourself go on random bunny trails, telling stories that don't matter in regards to your topic.**

<u>Asset 3</u> – Statistic (Example: 98% of people who move to Asheville move there because of the accepting community)
**Using statistics can be helpful. But sometimes they are boring. So make sure that the statistic, first of all, is actually true (by the way- this is not a real statistic I used here). And secondly, make sure that you don't spend a lot of time pointing to the statistic. Use it in a punchy, impacting way. You can even insert it into the middle of your personal story in asset 1. For example,** "The first time I ever visited Asheville I felt so accepted and welcomed by so many amazing strangers that immediately felt like long lost friends. By the way, did you know that 98% of people who move to Asheville do so because of the accepting community?

*When I heard that stat, it completely made sense to me. The next thing I knew, I found myself moving here for the same reason!"* **Do you see what I did there? I added a valuable asset to the story to prove the point, without putting all of my focus on that asset. I added a statistic that proved my sub-point without taking the focus off of the story.**

**Once you have inserted your Assets for your first Explanation then you can go on to your second and third Explanation and insert your Assets there as well. Basically, you want to have 3 or 4 sub points (explanations) filled with examples, stories, statistics, and supporting facts (assets) that all support your main Topic.**

The **Assets** section of preparation is also the section where we build out strong introduction and conclusion statements for your overall talk.

I like to come up with a killer first sentence and a

strong last sentence. Your opener has to be an attention getter. It tells people that you are there and you have something to say. Many people might not know who you are and that means that they will be immediately judging you.

I'm not trying to freak you out here, but I'm just being honest.

People want to know *does this person have anything worth listening to? Do they have anything worth saying that is worth my time? Or should I pull out my iPhone and scroll through social media for the next ½ hour?*

First of all, you do have something to say that is worth their time. So don't let that initial question intimidate you at all! If they are on their phone when you start speaking, they will set them down once you finish your first sentence- because you have something of value to say and you know it. People can feel it when a speaker knows that what they have to say actually matters. It's not only about your first sentence and the exact words that you say. But it's the way that you stand up, the way that you grab the mic, the way that you say the words. It all matters.

That doesn't mean that you need to overthink every move, it just means that you need to actually believe in yourself and be confident that the reason you are getting the microphone is because you are the person who was destined to have that microphone. The reason they are in the audience is because they were destined to hear from you. Get that in your head and you will be both humble and confident. And that is a powerful combination that will immediately **command attention without the need to insecurely demand it.**

With that said, here are a few suggestions for your introduction and conclusion.

## Introduction

I like to be very casual in my initial approach with an audience. I find that in most settings, this works very well. Whether it's a small meeting of 15-20 people listening to me, or a large meeting of 100 or more, I enjoy starting out my talk with everyone in the same way that I would meet a friend in my home.

"How is everyone doing?"

Then I stand there for about 3 seconds with a genuine smile on my face and wait for them to actually respond. I know it sounds a little funny- but trust me, it always works for me no matter how big the crowd is. It serves two purposes: 1) it shows people that I'm acknowledging their presence and I'm not there just to recite a speech but to actually interact and engage with them 2) it loosens people up and gets them actually thinking in an interactive way. Obviously, you don't have to copy my exact phrase here. But the principle is the same- let them know that you see them, you are there with them, and you want to actually connect with them and not just talk at them.

After the initial phrase or interaction with the crowd I like to say something humorous based on something I've noticed about the audience or about the city that I'm in. Or I say something funny based on an interaction that I've had with someone in the crowd. I never demean anyone. Instead, pull out a random fact or short funny story that will help loosen people up.

What's my rationale in this?

As soon as most people sit down to listen to a public speech (unless it's at a comedy club or a speaker that they are very familiar with) they get super uptight and serious. Guess what kind of atmosphere that creates? Ugh. Terribly boring and awfully uncomfortable.

So I like to find a tasteful way to lighten up the mood depending on the setting that I'm in. Tell a joke that relates to your crowd and always be aware of the cultural context of the crowd. You don't want to tell an off-color joke if the majority of your crowd is religious. I totally understand the power of shock-value, but I also don't want to shock the majority of my listeners to the point of leaving the room or tuning out the rest of my speech (which is the most valuable part of the speech anyway).

Here's an example of something I might say to start a talk-

"How's everyone doing this afternoon?" No response-

"That bad, huh?" Then I smile and chuckle a bit.

This gets people laughing or at least smirking.

"Well, it's great to be here with you all. I love speaking in _____ city. It's such a beautiful place! I get blown away by the view from _____ road- it's absolutely breathtaking. I seriously love the sight seeing. There's never a dull moment. In fact, I think I saw a male nun riding a unicycle on my way here today. Seriously, so amazing. How many of you have seen that guy?" Then I wait for a few hands to go up and acknowledge them... "Interesting guy right? As soon as I saw that guy, I knew that this was my kind of city."

Okay- so I just did two things there: 1) I established a small bit of credibility with the crowd because I mentioned the beauty of the town and showed appreciation for something that they have appreciation for 2) I made a silly joke based off of a true story that happened to me earlier in the day- and people will know exactly what I'm talking about because they've probably seen that guy on the unicycle downtown. Whether they like it or not, it's a funny thing and it will at least get a few giggles out of them.

Also, I'm not trying to be hilarious. I'm just pointing out something that actually is pretty hilarious. I discourage looking up "good jokes to use in your speech" on Google- it's just a bad idea in my opinion. Use Yahoo instead.

Totally kidding.

Anyway, back to my example.

So- I point out a funny thing that the audience knows about. And suddenly, we somehow feel connected. The crowd and the speaker are chatting. *How are you guys doing? I love your city and I love your weird unicycle nun-guy.* And suddenly some people like me already.

While some think I tell crappy jokes. And others are annoyed that I'm trying to build rapport with them and won't be so easily won over. But, at least they will be impressed by the fact that I'm confident, I know my introduction, and I'm not only speaking at them, but also pressing them to interact with me. They either like me a lot already, or they are open to the idea and ready to hear more.

Then I begin with my introductory line: *"We all have a calling and a destiny that we were created to fulfill, but not everyone is willing to go through the struggle of finding and fulfilling that destiny."*

Or I start with a story that launches into my topic. For example, *"Five years ago I was living on my friends couch, eating Roman Noodles for lunch and dinner, feeling like I was headed no where. I realized that if I continued the way I was going, that I would be unfulfilled for the rest of my life. Jobless, nearly homeless, and with little to no vision for my life. That's when I made the choice to figure out what I was born to do and start taking steps towards making that dream come true. We all have a calling and a destiny that we were created to fulfill, but not everyone is willing to go through the struggle of finding and fulfilling that destiny."*

I launched into a story that caught people's attention. It's personal and it's actually an **Asset** to build up my main point. It's got shock value as well since there is such an extreme difference in standing in front of people as a public speaker to sleeping on a friends couch eating Roman Noodles. (This isn't my story, by the way. I didn't live on my friends couch. But I did eat way too many Roman Noodles in college.)

Remember, **Assets** can be used anywhere in a public speech. They are stories, quotes, and other details that can be sprinkled throughout the speech to add value and support to the main point. Your introduction is actually an **Asset** that builds towards your explanations/sub-points of your talk. It's the first thing that people hear form you. Make it solid and make it count.

## Conclusion

Some folks over complicate the conclusion and freak out about it. They genuinely think that this is what everyone will remember from their speech. That's actually not true- as long as your content was killer, your conclusion can be very simple and you will be just fine.

But if your content is amazing, then why not make your conclusion equally amazing?

I like to make my conclusion short, sweet, and powerful; sometimes using it to recap my **Explanation**/sub-points very concisely and then driving home my **Topic**/main point with intensity and passion.

Think of your conclusion like it's your last chance to put the capstone on the building. You've just built up your **Topic** for the last 20-45 minutes and now you are concluding with something that will drive home the power of your main point.

Again, just as in my introduction, I like to end

with a story.

**Storytelling is powerful and it gets people's attention.**

There is something about a story that makes us stop what we are doing or thinking about and tune in to listen.

*Facts speak to our heads.*

*Stories speak to our hearts.*

I highly recommend using a personal story or a story that you've read or heard that concerns your main topic. Use something that pulls on people's heartstrings; something that stirs their emotions and will make them tear up, or get passionate about the topic at hand.

This is NOT manipulation.

This is good communication.

A bad communicator only appeals to logic.

A good communicator appeals to logic and emotion.

We are emotional beings and we need that reality to be involved in our communication and our listening experience.

We want to stir the hearts of people in these final moments so that they are driven to do something about what they have just heard.

Here is an example of a conclusion that I might use:

*"I want to close with this. Last year I was with my grandfather before he died and I asked him while on his deathbed- 'Grandpa, what is the one piece of life advice you want to give me?' You know what he said? He said, 'Son, when I was in my 20's I had a dream to be a doctor. But I never thought I would be able to accomplish that dream because I wasn't good at school. I let negative thoughts and the fear of failure keep me from following my dream. I'm a happy man- I had a good life and an amazing family; and we were always provided for, but I feel that I was missing something major in my life. I always regretted not following my heart and going for my dream. Son, whatever it takes, find out your calling and go make it happen.' I want to challenge you all with this statement today- Find out your calling and don't let anything stop you. Whatever it takes, let's go make it happen. Let's be the generation who knows what we were*

*made for, dreams big, and accomplishes those dreams. Thank you."*

Did you feel that? It kind of inspired me. And I'm the one who made up the story! That's the power of using a strong story as an **Asset** at the end of your conclusion.

This story can be sad, funny, or anything. But you want to finish with a story and/or a statistic that pulls on people's emotions. And then spend time recapping your main point and encouraging people to leave your speech with a goal in mind. Your talk should challenge them to think differently and act differently. So remind them of that and challenge them to put into practice what you have just spoken about.

## Master the Speech

This is the final step in your message preparation.

This is the part where you practice your talk over and over until you feel confident and secure about it.

You should practice enough so that if you are

asked what your **Topic** is and what your **Explanations** are you would be able to tell people without skipping a beat.

A quick note about sound amplification: I encourage my students to hold an object and practice speaking into it like a microphone. I usually give them a wooden spoon or something like that. It really doesn't matter what you use, as long as it's something around the size of a microphone. I'd encourage you to hold the microphone a softball's width away from your mouth while speaking. Different sound systems will vary, so show up early to your actual speaking location and make sure to do a sound test with your sound guy. If you don't have a sound system, then make sure to speak from your gut and not your throat so you don't lose your voice. I like to use breathing exercises from vocal instructors. You can find online vocal instructors with a quick search on YouTube if you're interested.

Here are a few tips for you during this stage of **Mastering** your speech:

## 1. Practice Your Transitions

How are you going to make the change from **Explanation** one to **Explanation** two? You don't have to say, *My first point is* _____ – in fact, I'd encourage you not to do that. Instead, I'd suggest just going straight from your intro and saying something to the effect of, *"In order to find our calling and destiny in life we must first* _____.*"*

With that statement, we just established our topic in people's minds and gave them the first **Explanation** or sub-point without saying *My topic today is* _____ or *my first point is* _____.

Create <u>simple transitions</u> between each **Explanation** that will help you move smoothly from one sub-point to the next without being too mechanical about it. People are smart. They will realize that you have three points by the way you communicate your sub-points/**Explanations** to them during the talk.

## 2. Place Memory Markers Along the Road of Your Speech

For instance, use some of your **Assets** as memory markers for you. If you lose your place, ask yourself (in your own mind), *Have I told the story about _____ yet?* Or *Have I shared the statistic about _____ yet?* Stories, quotes, and statistics are easy to remember. If you can remember your **Assets** then that will help you find your place within the talk if you get lost and are not using note cards.

That brings us to another point- notes.

**3. Use Notes!**

Almost every speaker does.

But don't write out your entire speech. That can become way too mechanical.

I have seen people get on stage with 10 pages full of typed out notes. It looked like they had written a long English paper. When they got lost in their memory, they would refer to their "notes" only to shuffle through them looking for their spot. Even though the information and content they shared was powerful, the stack of paper in their hand was very distracting.

Notes can be your best friend or your worst enemy. The difference will be how you write them and if you can refer to them without causing a scene. I'd suggest writing them on an iPad or a small smart phone. Write down the skeleton outline for your talk.

Write out your shortened version of your **Intro** with **Assets** included in it. Then write out your explanations in bullet form and leave a lot of space in between them for your main **Assets** to be put in short-hand form. Then throw in a shortened version of your conclusion at the end.

Here's a quick example of what my notes might look like if I was talking about **"Finding and Fulfilling Your Destiny"**

Intro: How's everyone doing? Joke about Nun on Bike. Story about how I used to live on couch eating Roman now I know my calling.

Explanation 1- Everyone has a Calling

Asset 1 – quote from John Smith

Asset 2 – story about Jim and Zach

Explanation 2- Your calling should be your passion

Asset 1 – stat about gen x'ers not enjoying their jobs

Asset 2 – Story of man who turned his passion into a carreer

Asset 3 – Quote by Jane Fonda

Explanation 3 – Whatever it takes

Asset 1 – quote by John Madden "Every can accomplish their dreams"

Asset 2 – Statistic about millennials thinking outside the box about their careers

Asset 3 – story of man who walked 1,000 miles to reach his goal- this is how determined we should be to find and fulfill our calling

Conclusion – story about Grandpa

# 8 FINAL TIPS AND TRICKS

Once you have practiced your speech and have your content drilled into your brain then you have done most of the hard work.

The next step is to actually get up there and present yourself in a relaxed and comfortable manner. Here are a few tips and tricks that I have learned over the years that help me deliver a killer talk no matter how many people are in attendance. And no, I'm not going to say "Picture your audience naked."

### What to Do When I Forget Where I Am in My Talk?

First of all, we all get a little lost at certain points when we deliver a speech. It's normal. That's why we have notes. Take a moment, look down at your notes, find your place, and get going again.

## Know this- that a moment of silence is not the end of the world!

When you are in front of people, 3 seconds of silence can feel like an eternity. But if you play it cool and just relax, then people will genuinely think it was a dramatic pause for effect. Or they will think you just had to gather your thoughts for a moment. Or they will think that you just needed to grab a drink of water from the podium. Don't worry! Your mind will tell you all kinds of things in that three second time lapse- *"Oh no, I forgot where I am! Everyone is staring at me! I must look like an idiot! Do I have a booger? Did I leave my stove on? Oh God, why me?"* Yes, all of that will run through your head in 3 seconds. Just take a deep breath, check your notes, and hop back on topic.

Just tell yourself the truth- *"I've got this. Remember what I practiced, check my notes, and keep trucking forward. This is going to change people's lives!"*

I like to simply stop, take a deep breath (literally, I take a breath), look around the room or at the back of the room, look down at my notes for a moment, then say a transition statement like, "I love this next point." Or "I'm reminded of a story..." then I dive into one of my stories/ **Assets.**

Just remember, the pause is never as long as it feels. People are usually not thinking what you think they are thinking. It doesn't matter if you just messed up a word or a phrase, it only matters that you relax and jump right back on topic.

### *What if I get nervous?*

A random trick that I use when I get nervous is this: I find a location in the back of the room that I will stare at for about 3 seconds. I will look about 3 inches over the heads of the people and stare at the back wall.

I know- that sounds ***super weird***. But trust me, it works.

**Most people, when they get nervous or lost in their speech will stare at the ground** and say,

"Uh, um… and uh…." and nervously giggle and turn red or something.

But looking down at the ground is a HUGE NO-NO when speaking!

**Say this with me "DO NOT LOOK AT THE GROUND!"**

When someone looks at the ground it immediately shows that they are lost, don't know what they are saying, and they are trying to come up with something to cover the fact that they are lost.

But when someone looks up, it shows that they are trying to remember info that is already inside of them. Not making up something new. It gives off a vibe of confidence and control.

Often times, people won't actually be able to tell that you are looking **above** their heads. They will think you are looking at the person behind them and still engaging with the audience. But if you look down, they will know that you are only talking to your feet, the floor, and the bugs. It's a quick way for your crowd to lose confidence in you.

When doing private consulting with speakers,

this is one of the main things I work with them on. I am consistently saying "Look at the wall behind me, take a deep breath, gather your thoughts, and keep going- **you know exactly where you are."**

This is HUGE: *__Most people don't actually forget their content. Instead, they get nervous about what their listeners are thinking about them in that moment and their nerves get the better of them.__*

Instead of staring deep into the eyes of people when you are trying to recall your content, look up a bit towards the back wall, almost as an act of looking up into your brain, find the content (because it's there) and keep going. You've got this! Looking up will show confidence and control and most people won't notice it at all (unless you spend the whole speech staring at the back wall which is probably not a good idea).

## What do I do if someone is looking at me funny?

Don't worry about it. Seriously. Do not get into a staring contest with someone! That will make it awkward for you and for that person. Remember, you cannot read their thoughts. You'll see someone staring at you with a strange blank stare on his or her face and of course, it must be the fact that your speech is terrible, right? Or you must have something in your teeth? Or maybe you said something that offended them?

But the truth is, they probably just read a text message from a friend and are trying to think of how to respond, while also trying to ignore the text and listen to you. Or, they actually just look like that. It happens.

You don't have to figure out what they are thinking. <u>Instead of focusing on what they might be thinking, influence their thinking by confidently continuing your speech.</u>

Simply look at a different person in the crowd who seems more engaged and keep your mind focused on communicating your message.

### *Practice, Practice, Practice!!!*

Practice doesn't make perfect, but it does bring peace.

After almost 18 years of public speaking, I still get nervous before I get on stage. But it is a good nervous. It means that I'm excited about what I get to do and that I take it seriously! But not too seriously. I realize that I am just a mouthpiece, a conduit of sorts, for a story that will bring encouragement to others. My job is to do my best to be honest in my approach, excellent in my presentation, and have a good time.

If I will take the time to prepare and practice then it will actually enhance my ability to be relaxed and have fun while up there. One of the best ways I like to practice is by actually thinking about my topic for weeks in advance. I think about it, meditate on it, bring it up in conversation with others, and let it be something that resonates in my mind and heart for days or weeks leading up to the event. In this way, I am getting the topic well oiled in my mind and ready at a moments notice to share my thoughts on it.

My wife will always ask me if I've prepared my talk. And I usually tell her that I'm always preparing. It's kind of our little joke. Really, I'm only halfway joking, but halfway serious. I really do live in my head for weeks when I'm planning a talk. I think on it, write down little notes, and pay attention to things around me for stories and quotes that will be useful to my topic.

One thing I like to do with my one on one student's is to have them practice their entire talk in front of me. That way I can coach them on their transitions and their presentation. I'd encourage you to record your talk with your smart phone or another recording device. Find a closed room and then deliver your talk to your recording device a few different times- then go back and listen to it. Practice telling your stories and going through your transitions from one point to the next (out loud). This will make you more comfortable with your content and cement it into your memory.

Well, that's all I've got for you! (So much for an amazing conclusion). If you're interested in gaining more training for public speaking then visit blaiseforet.com/chattingwith100 and check out my communications course.

Good luck and go change the world!

# CHATTING WITH 100

www.ingramcontent.com/pod-product-compliance
Lightning Source LLC
Chambersburg PA
CBHW070329190526
45169CB00005B/1805